The "Rimas" of Gustavo A. Becquer

You are holding a reproduction of an original work that is in the public domain in the United States of America, and possibly other countries. You may freely copy and distribute this work as no entity (individual or corporate) has a copyright on the body of the work. This book may contain prior copyright references, and library stamps (as most of these works were scanned from library copies). These have been scanned and retained as part of the historical artifact.

This book may have occasional imperfections such as missing or blurred pages, poor pictures, errant marks, etc. that were either part of the original artifact, or were introduced by the scanning process. We believe this work is culturally important, and despite the imperfections, have elected to bring it back into print as part of our continuing commitment to the preservation of printed works worldwide. We appreciate your understanding of the imperfections in the preservation process, and hope you enjoy this valuable book.

❊ ❊ ❊

This is an authorized facsimile of the original book, and was produced in 1970 by microfilm-xerography by University Microfilms, A Xerox Company, Ann Arbor, Michigan, U.S.A.

❊ ❊ ❊

The "Rimas" of Gustavo A. Becquer

Translated by Jules Renard

BOSTON: RICHARD G. BADGER
The Gorham Press
1908

868
B4r
tR4
1908a

Copyright, 1908, by Richard G. Badger

[All Rights Reserved.]

The Gorham Press, Boston, U.S.A.

*This work
became a possibility through the
intelligent and sympathetic co-operation of*
CORDELIA M. THIEL
and is therefore fitly dedicated to her by
The Translator

PREFACE

In submitting a translation of the celebrated Rimas of Gustavo A. Becquer for publication, I do so without absolute knowledge as to whether this task was ever before attempted in the English language. Beyond a solitary translation of "Las Golondrinas," I have never seen nor heard of an English translation of this famous collection, and the gentleman who originally called my attention to the beauties of Becquer in the original, himself a Spanish scholar of very high order and a man of wide acquaintance with Spanish literature, assured me that he never had known of an English translation of Becquer's Rimas and doubted whether it were possible.

If ever a literary work was undertaken in a spirit of fondness for its subject, this translation certainly has been, and if the publication of this collection does not meet with the instantaneous recognition which the original demands, I shall have to admit that for me at least, it is an impossibility to reproduce the spirit of the Spanish poet.

The Rimas of Becquer, while never intended by the author as a perfect work on which his fame might rest, have been judged by posterity to be worthy of the highest recognition and have become a household word in both hemispheres wherever the Spanish language is spoken by cultivated people.

I have felt all along that in attempting this task I had undertaken a very hazardous proposition. The muse of Becquer is so delicately suggestive, so epigrammatic and so concentrated and concise that it must be the despair of every translator who uses any other language than those directly derived from the classics like the original. A perfect translation of Becquer in English, I myself believe to be an utter impossibility. I have found passages in the different Rimas which could not be reproduced literally without detriment to the author's spirit, and certain modifications will therefore be found which can only be deemed excusable for this reason. I have, however, in the entire collection, whenever the option was given to me of deciding between a reproduction of the author's letter and his spirit, invariably given my preference to the latter. This I believe to be the highest aim of the translator. I have not even followed punctiliously the meter laid down in the original, because I have found that in many cases the English language does not readily adapt itself to an exact reproduction; and in rhyme I was confronted with the additional difficulty, that the assonant rhyme, so largely used by all the Spanish writers, is incapable of being conveyed properly in any of the Northern tongues. Therefore, beyond a few specimens which I have chosen to translate in blank verse, I have adopted the policy all through of substituting rhymes as nearly perfect as possible for Becquer's assonant rhymes, in the supposition that this substitution would be more satisfactory to English ears, who have not been trained in the intricacies of the assonant rhyme.

I feel that even in an abortive way I have rendered some service to the Anglo-Saxon race, by familiarizing them with the poetical works of Becquer, who may well be classed as one of the models of lyrical poets. If I have succeeded even partially in conveying the spirit of the great original to prospective readers, I shall feel that a work which was begun purely as a labor of love, has also met with an ample reward.

THE TRANSLATOR.

SEATTLE, WASHINGTON, 1907.

THE "RIMAS" OF
GUSTAVO A. BECQUER

I

I know a hymn, titanical and strange
Which to the spirit's night proclaims the dawn;
These pages are its final cadences
Spread out among the shadows by the air.

How gladly would I note it, if I could
Subdue the plain, rebellious speech of man
With words, which would be sighs and smiles at
 once,
Colors and notes as fitting characters.

Vain is the struggle! — For there is no form
Which may enshrine it. Scarcely, beauteous one,
May I, on hearing it, sing it for thee,
Alone and holding thy dear hands in mine.

II

A rapid-flying dart, by Fate impelled
  For blind destruction and which cannot know
Where it may find its quivering course repelled,
  Nor why it strikes the blow.

A withered leaf, stripped from a famished tree
  By frenzied autumn-gales in madd'ning dance;
What ditch may shelter its extremity
  Is hid in ignorance.

A monstrous billow, which the ocean wind
  Curls and drives onward, lashes into foam;
Rolling, unheedful of what shore may find
  For it a restful home.

A waxlight, flick'ring in a chandelier,
  Which, ere it is extinguished, sputters low;
Which is the first to end its brief career
  And which the last to go?

All these am I, — With blind, hap-hazard aim
  I cross this world, without the slightest heed
From what mysterious origin I came,
  Nor where my steps may lead.

III

Like Indian hurricane
  Lending its impetus
To lash the ocean-main;
Stirring the sluggish brain,
  — A quickening incubus.

Murmurs, which in the soul
  Rise and increase in ire,
With hoarse announcement roll
Deep in the crater's bowl,
  — Like a volcano's fire.

Mis-shapen silhouettes
  Of non-existing things;
Landscapes, that one forgets,
Seen, as through gauzy nets
  Or magic mirrorings.

Colors, which blending, glow
  Within the air; the bright
Atoms to atoms grow
Till the celestial bow
  Swims in prismatic light.

Words of all meaning shorn,
  Sense, quite bereft of words;
Cadences rudely torn
From rhythm, measure, norm,
  — Like broken potter's sherds.

Mem'ries and vain desires
   For things we ne'er have known;
Joy, which the fancy fires,
Tears that the heart requires
   — When we're alone.

Nervous activity
   Seeking to find a mean
For some utility;
Steed of high quality
   Without a guiding rein.

Madness, that steeps the soul
   In fierce elation;
Draughts from celestial bowl,
Creative genius as a whole, —
   — This is inspiration.

Tremendous voice, which regulates
   The chaos of the brain;
Which lowering shadows dissipates,
   Restoring light again.

Resplendent rein of gold, to curb
   With power the flying steed,
When frantic fancies him disturb
   And he is deaf to heed.

Refulgent thread of light, which binds
   In fagots our strewn thought;
Sun, which in vaulted zenith shines,
   Breaking through clouds, as naught.

Discerning hand, persisting e'er
  To re-unite and bring
Our untamed words within a rare
  And richly jewelled ring.

Harmonious rhythm, which confines
  Within a certain bound
The fleeting notes and deftly twines
  A measured cadence round.

Chisel, which bites the sculptor's block,
  Uniting in this duty
Ideals, which our senses mock
  With perfect plastic beauty.

The region, where in ordered troops
  Ideas may revolve;
Where atoms form concentric groups
  From secret, joint resolve.

Pellucid spring, whose balmy waves
  Assuage the thirst of fever;
Oasis, which the spirit craves
  As vigor's best retriever.

Such is our reason.

Forever battling with them, stroke for stroke,
  Forever conqueror of both, — no one
Can bring them both beneath a common yoke
  Except the force of genius alone.

pellucid : translucent, not of[f] clear

IV

O, do not tell me, that, its treasure, spent,
The lyre is mute from lack of argument,
We may not always rich in poets be,
But never destitute of poesy.

While billows are inflamed with blushes bright
And tremble to receive the kiss of light;
While Phœbus may in majesty behold
The scattered clouds of purple fire and gold;

While in its bosom's folds, the atmosphere
Rare perfumes and sweet harmonies may bear,
While spring exists to fill the heart with glee
There will be always, always, poesy.

While science may not, of endeavor rife,
Discover the true origin of life;
While chasms still remain in sea or sky,
Which all our calculations may defy;

And, while humanity in darkness stalks,
Advancing, without knowing, where it walks,
While there is left a single mystery,
There will be always, always, poesy.

While we may feel the soul rejoicing, while
Our lips do not endorse it with a smile;
While we may weep in silent misery
Without a single tear to dew the eye;

While heart and head, by adverse forces pricked,
To useless strife, continue to conflict;
While hopes and recollections still may be,
There will be always, always, poesy.

While there are eyes, which may reflect the gaze
Of other eyes in sympathetic rays;
While one lip still with longing may reply
Unto another's corresponding sigh;

While two souls may confound in mutual bliss
And seal the compact with a fervent kiss;
While one fair woman lives for you and me,
There will be always, always, poesy!

V

A subtle essence indefinable
  Am I, a being without form or frame;
Within no certain bounds assignable,
  A vital spirit, yet without a name.

I swim within a void immensurate,
  I tremble in the radii of the sun,
Among the shades I love to palpitate,
  The clouds and I together float as one.

I am the slender ray of golden light
  Emitted by the distant evening star;
I am the radiance, serene and bright
  Which gentle moonbeams send us from afar.

I am the gorgeous, ruby-tinted cloud
  Which sinks at eventide, into the sea;
I am the errant comets sweeping, proud,
  And luminous appendage equally.

I am the snow upon the mountain peak,
  I am the glow upon the desert-sand;
I am the blue waves of the sea and eke,
  I am the foam upon the water's strand.

Within each hymn of praise I am a note,
  The violet's fragrance I personify;
The fleeting marsh-light in a tomb or moat,
  The trailing ivy on the ruins high.

I thunder in the torrent's headlong course,
  I hiss in the electric spark of fire;

I blind you in the lightning's awful force,
   I groan amid the torture, stern and dire.

I laugh in Nature's multi-peopled choir,
   I whisper in the waving blades of grass;
Within the curling billows I suspire,
   And weep in shrivelled autumn-leaves, that pass.

I vibrate in the atoms, which comprise
   The wreath of smoke, which from the earth ascends,
We see it gently toward the sky arise
   In spiral form, contorted and immense.

I mingle in the filmy golden threads
   Which insect artisans so well construct,
When the siesta claims our wearied heads
   Among the trees, which to repose conduct.

The flying nymphs I eagerly pursue
   While they, disrobed, are sporting in the cool,
Refreshing current, hidden from all view,
   Within the shelter of the crystal pool.

I follow up, upon the ocean's bed
   Light footed naiads, merry, winsome girls,
Where coral woods are richly carpeted
   With an array of dazzling, snow-white pearls.

I mingle with the subterranean gnomes
   In hollow caverns, far from solar ray,
Behold the wondrous riches of their homes,
   Where gems create an artificial day.

I seek the trace of foot prints, now erased
   From former ages, which have ceased to be;
I know of empires, which have been displaced,
   Of whom no name remains, nor history.

Before me are in dizzy whirls unrolled,
   Revolving worlds in silent majesty;
Such is my vision, that I may behold
   The whole creation with observant eye.

I know of regions, nebulous, remote,
   Where even sound has failed to penetrate;
Where stars in embryotic chaos float
   And eagerly the breath of life await.

I am the wondrous bridge which dares to cross
   The bottomless abyss by Titans riven;
I am the unknown ladder o'er the foss
   Which re-unites the realms of earth and heaven.

I am the ring of potency enorm,
   Unseen, yet subjugating, as it ought,
The grosser world of mere external form
   Unto the elevated world of thought.

I am, at last that latent quality,
   That unknown essence, spiritual haze,
That perfume, delicate in mystery
   Of which the poet is the fitting vase.

VI

As wanders o'er a darkened field of blood,
  Refreshing to the sense, a gentle breeze
In night and silence, with a grateful flood
  Of perfumes fraught and pleasing harmonies,

So may we see the sweet Ophelia pass
  Within the British poet's awful play,
Symbolical of grief and tenderness,
  With songs and strewing flowers on her way.

VII

In a corner full of gloom
Of the formal drawing room,
Prey to dust and silence, we
The neglected harp may see;
Melancholy seems its lot,
Of its owner quite forgot.

Notes lie dormant in its strings
Just as in the bird, who clings
To the branches, while asleep;
They await the welcome sweep
Of the snowy hands, whose skill
May invoke them at her will.

"Oh, how frequently," thought I,
"Genius thus asleep may lie
"And, like Lazarus, await
"The desired, portentous date,
"When the voice shall sweetly say:
"'Rise thou and pursue thy way!'"

VIII

When I behold the blue horizon merge
  And lose itself afar within a gauze
Of restless, golden dust, my fancies urge,
  That I could break all ordinary laws
And it seems possible to tear away
  My eager spirit from this wretched clay,
To float with golden mists, dissolved in bright
  And myriad atoms of celestial light.

When I behold, at night, the trembling stars
  Within the dark recesses of the sky,
So that my fancy vividly compares
  Their lustre with an ardent, burning eye,
It then seems possible to wing in flight
  To where they shine and bathe within their light,
To kindle with them in a blazing sea
  And in a kiss confound identity.

Although within a sea of doubt I plash
  And spurn beliefs, which with my reason clash,
Yet they proclaim, these anxious doubts of mine,
  A certain trace of origin divine.

IX

The softly-moaning breezes kiss the wavelets, while at play,
As they curl in undulations with a restless revelry;
The sun bestows a kiss upon the cloud-banks in the West,
While gold and purple brilliancy their neutral tints invest;
The flame around a burning log is ardent in its aim
To glide with motion serpentine to kiss another flame;
The willow, even, bends its weight down to the longing stream
And gives its contribution to the universal theme.

X

The unseen atoms of the air,
   Inflamed, are dancing round about;
The sky dissolves in flashes rare
   Of trembling gold, a dazzling rout;
The earth appears with rapture buoyed
   And vibrates, as if overjoyed;
The sounds come stealing o'er to me
   Of strange, delightful harmony;
I hear the sound of kisses, — feel
   The fluttering of wings, — I reel
And close my eyelids! — Who is nigh?
   — 'T is Eros, who is passing by.

XI

I am ardent, I am brown,
Me the fiery passions crown;
I am eager to decoy
Thee into the realms of joy,
Do I please thy fancy? — Speak!
— Nay; it is not thee I seek.

Delicate my brow and fair,
Wreathed with coils of golden hair;
And I guard a limitless
Treasure-trove of tenderness.
Do I please thy fancy? — Speak!
— Nay; it is not thee I seek.

Like a lightning-flash I gleam
Or a wild, phantastic dream;
Bodiless, impossible
Fleeting and intangible;
No one could my feelings move!
— O, then come! — Be thou my love!

XII

Because your eyes are colored like the sea,
  Do not complain, my child!
The naiads use such eyes in wanton glee
  And sportive gambols wild;
Minerva's eye of green a source of power is
Green are the pupils of the prophet's houris.

Green is the color of the woods in spring;
  Among its other dyes
It is displayed within the rainbow's ring,
  With it the emerald vies;
Green are the ocean-billows, green the sorrel,
Green are our hopes and green the poet's laurel.

Your cheek is like the carmine of the rose,
  Sprinkled with pearls of frost,
When it before its proper season glows
  To lead, at any cost.
But do not fear! It is the merest fancy
That your eyes mar it! Everybody can see
That they are like the early almond leaves,
Humid and restless, when a zephyr breathes.

Your mouth is like the ruby-purple tint
  Which we admire in burst
And ripe pomegranates, with their luscious hint
  How well they quench our thirst.
But, none the less, esteem it as a fancy
That your eyes spoil it! Everybody can see,
Angered, they sparkle like the waves, which roar
Against the perilous Cantabrian shore.

Your forehead, where the golden curls are massed,
  Is like a snowy peak,
Whereon the sun may linger, with its last
  Declining rays, oblique.
Be not alarmed! It is an idle fancy
That your eyes mar it! Everybody can see,
That they are like a brooch of emerald rare,
Clasping the ermine of your skin and hair.

XIII

Blue is your pupil and whene'er you smile
  Its softened clarity recalls to me
The trembling radiance of the morning, while
  Its splendors are reflected in the sea.

Blue is your pupil and whene'er you weep
  Transparent tears, like dainty jewels set
Appear to me, as they unbidden creep,
  Like drops of dew upon a violet.

Blue is your pupil and when I descry
  Like points of light, ideas radiate
Within its depth, it seems to scintillate
  Like some lost pleiad in the evening sky.

XIV

I saw you for an instant
   As if by breezes blown;
The image of your eyes remained
   Imprisoned in my own.
Like dusky blots encircled
   With fire, that dazzle one
And seem to blind our vision
   While gazing at the sun.

Relentlessly pursuing
   Wherever I may gaze,
I see their pupils follow me
   With a devouring blaze;
It is not you, who troubles me,
   The rest I could ignore;
It is your look, which haunts me,
   Your eyes and nothing more.

In the corner of my alcove
   With wild disordered stare
I see them glowing, fixed on me
   In a fantastic glare.
And when I sleep, I feel them
   Hover above and glow,
Awaiting the occasion
   To lay their victim low.

I've heard of exhalations
   Illuminating gloom,
Which lead the trusting wand'rer
   Unto a wretched doom;

I feel myself drawn onward
As by an under-tow,
But where your eyes will lead me:
Alas, I do not know.

XV

Floating wreath of wintry light,
　Curling belt of snowy foam,
Sound sonorous of the bright
　Harp of gold within the home,
Kiss of zephyrs, wave of light,
　　— This art thou!

Thou airy shade, that vanishest whenever
I seek to touch thee in a vain endeavor,
Like flick'ring flames, like sound, like fog opaque,
Like gentle murmurs from the azure lake.

Sounding billow on a shoreless sea,
Errant comet in vacuity,
Long-drawn, labored wail
Of the hoarse-voiced gale,
Keen desire for better things to be,
　　— This am I!

I, who in my agony alway
Turn my eyes to thine by night and day;
I, who madly, tirelessly pursue
Mocking shadows, hollow phantoms, who
To my unavailing efforts seem
Like the offspring of a fevered dream.

XVI

If, at the stirring of the sweet bluebells
  Upon thy balcony, — thou dost believe,
  That murm'ring breezes in their passage grieve
And melancholy them to sighs impels, —
Know then, that it is I,
Who lurk amid their foliage and sigh.

If, at the bearing of a sound confused
  From distant noises, thou dost seem to hear,
  That far-off voices urgently appear
To call thee by the name, — be not abused,
— For it is I, who call
From where the deep surrounding shadows fall.

If, in the deep tranquility of night
  Thy heart is troubled with disturbing fear
  At feeling on thy lips, or hovering near
A parching respiration, — banish fright,
Know thou, that I abide
And breathe, unseen, at thy beloved side.

XVII

To-day the earth, to-day the heavens smile,
  To-day the sun has reached its highest goal
  And probed into the bottom of my soul:
To-day I saw her for a little while. —
  I saw my loved one and she glanced at me;
  To-day I do believe there is a Deity,

XVIII

Fatigued from the excitement of the ball,
  With hurried breath and flushed complexion, she,
  Sustained upon my arm, withdrew with me
In the remotest corner of the hall.

The light, diaphanous and silken tulle
  Beneath whose folds the restless bosom heaved,
  Sustained a flower, of its stalk bereaved,
In measured movement and rhythmitic rule.

As in an ivory cradle, which the sea
  Might gently rock, while zephyrs it caress,
  It slept in sweet, unconscious happiness,
Fanned by her breathing's regularity.

Immeasurable bliss! A joy supreme,
  Our whole existence in such task to steep!
  Ah, if the flowers have the power to sleep,
How rarely exquisite must be their dream!

XIX

When you incline your melancholy brow
Upon your swelling breast, you seem to me
A lily cut before maturity;
For God made an irrevocable vow,
That he would give you that chaste purity
Known as the lily's symbol, and that we
Might fully realize His great intent
And that you might His wisdom represent,
He placed His mark indelible to show
And made you, like the flower, of gold and sown.

XX

Know thou, that when at times thy red lips sear,
Like parching fires, the unseen atmosphere,
That souls, whose eyes can speak, may too, per-
    chance,
Kiss with a glance.

XXI

"What is poesy," you ask
   While you fix your pupil blue
On my own. — An easy task
   To reply; but why should you
Put this question unto me?
   — You, yourself, are poesy.

XXII

How is it possible, that roses could
Live in thy heart's impassioned neighborhood?
Ne'er have I seen until the present hour
A dread volcano to produce a flower.

XXIII

I'd give a world for just one glance from thee;
A heaven for a smile were paltry fee;
While for a kiss, — I do not know, what I
Would for a kiss consider equity.

XXIV

Two red tongues of fire about the same
  Woodland log entwining, which are seen
Kissing, as they form a single flame,
  Sinuous in motion, serpentine.

Two accords of praise, which at one time
  Wrested by the hand, approach in space
Forming to a suave, melodious chime
  Melting in harmonious embrace,

Billows, which together land, to share
  Common death upon the shelving ground
Which, in breaking up, still proudly wear
  Silver helmets on their crests encrowned.

Wreaths of misty vapor, which arise
  From the surface of the lake and vowed
To unite within the vasty skies,
  Merging in a single, snowy cloud.

Two deep kisses, which together sound,
  Two ideas, which one birth unrolls,
Two keen echoes, which themselves confound,
  Two such twin-conceptions are our souls.

XXV

When thee, at night, sleep's gauzy wings enfold
  And thy spread eyelids seem like ebon bows,
To listen to thy heart-throbs uncontrolled
  And bear upon my breast, thy head in deep
    repose —
I'd gladly give my soul
  Whatever I possess:
The light, the air, my dole
  Of thought and consciousness!

When thy eyes fix their gaze on things unseen
  And some reflected smile thy lips illumes,
To read the silent thought within thy mien,
  As o'er the sea's broad mirror pass the clouded
    fumes —
I'd gladly give my soul
  Whatever I desire:
Fame, glory, wealth, the whole
  Of genius' brilliant fire!

When mute thy tongue and breathing is oppressed,
  Thy black eye rolling and thy cheek inflamed,
To see between thy lashes, thy unrest
  Emit volcanic sparks from thy desires untamed,
I'd gladly give my soul
  Whate'er I hope for most
My faith, my spirit's goal,
  Of earth and heaven the host!

XXVI

In spite of selfish interest
Let it be frankly here confessed
That I with thee
Must quite agree
That odes are only good, when seen
Endorsed on bank-notes crisp and green. —
Some dolts will not be wanting, who
Will cross themselves with much ado
And vent their rank acerbity
Upon our nineteenth century,
Declaring modern women all
Prosaic and material. —
Such sentiments but serve to make
Four frozen poets run and quake,
When they essay in winter's ire
To wrap themselves within their lyre.
These are the dogs who bay their tune
To spite the poor, defenceless moon.
For you know well
And I can tell,
That there are very few of us
Who boast of real genius
While any booby may with gold
A world of poesy unfold.

XXVII

I tremble to look at thee, while awake;
But when asleep, a glance I dare to take;
Therefore I watch, while in enthrallment deep
O soul of my soul, thou art held by sleep.

Awakened, thou dost laugh, and thus, thy lips
Appear like restless, scarlet lightning tips
Dazzling and fitful in their zig-zag glow,
Coiled like a serpent on a sky of snow.

Asleep, the angle of thy mouth beguiles
With tender folds of reminiscent smiles,
Mild as the radiance, which the dying sun
Leaves in its wake, whene'er his course is run....
    Sleep thou!

Awakened, thou dost gaze and then thy eyes
With humid fire are glistening, such as lies
Upon the blue waves' crest, in mobile mounds
And which the sparkling sun by contact wounds. —

Asleep, across thy eye-lids thou dost shed
A tranquil brightness, constant, limited,
Just as a lamp's transparencies invite
Transmission of a tempered ray of light....
    Sleep thou!

Awakened, thou dost speak and speaking seem
Thy words vibrating a torrential stream
Or rain of pearls precipitately rolled
With clank and clatter in a cup of gold.

Asleep, I listen to thy measured flow
Of respiration, regular and low;
And hear a poem in its murmurs bland,
Which my enamored soul can understand....
    Sleep thou!

I place my hand above my heart, to still
Its restless beating, so that nothing will
Thy welcome and pacific slumbers blight,
And mar the solemn stillness of the night.

And now the shutters of thy balcony
I'll gently close, so that no curious ray
Of morning's dawning may seek entrance here
And with annoying brightness interfere....
    Sleep thou!

XXVIII

When a voice in dusky shadows hidden
  Murmurs and disturbs its mournful calm,
If I hear its echoings unbidden
  In my soul's recesses like a psalm;
Tell me: — Is it but the wind lamenting
  In its flurries madly circumventing,
Or may I interpret, that thy sigh
  Speaks to me of love in passing by?

When the red sun on my window glistens
  In the morn and love invokes thy shade,
If I feel with sensitive persistence
  How another mouth on mine is laid;
Tell me, is it but a frantic madness
  Blindly generated by my sadness,
Or else did thy heart, a true ally
  Waft to me a kiss within a sigh?

If, the brilliant day with night confounding,
  I, who love thee, seem so near to thee,
If, in every object me surrounding
  Proves thy presence its ubiquity;
Tell me: — Is my whole existence seeming,
  Do I touch and breathe while I am dreaming,
Or, in sighs transmitted, shall I think
  Thou hast given me thy breath to drink?

XXIX

Upon her lap she held an open book
  While furtively her black curls touched my
    cheek;
For all its letters not a passing look,
  In sultry silence no attempt to speak.—
How long we sat?—I did not know it then;
  I only know, that nothing but our breath
Was audible, escaping just as when
  Oppressed, it flies the shrivelled lips of death.—
I only know, that we both turned at once,
  Instinctively attracted, that our eyes
Sought, found each other like two flaming suns
  And that a kiss was heard in Paradise.

'T was Dante's "Hell," which we had both
    perused;
  When we resumed, I trembling said and low:
"Canst thou perceive intelligibly how
"A poem in one verse may be infused?"
  And, blushing, she replied: "I see it now."

XXX

A melting tear was rising in her eye
And to my lips argued an apology,
Deep, contrite, self-accusing; — but our pride
Banished the guardian angel from our side;
It dried her tear with its devouring blaze
And hushed was my conciliatory phrase.

She follows her path; I pursue my own,
Yet oft, when thinking of our love, alone,
Marvel, why I was silent on that day;
While she, perhaps, with saddened heart may say:
"Why did I not relent? — Alas, I reap
"My folly's harvest. Why did I not weep?"

XXXI

Our passion was a tragic comedy
   In whose incongruous and grotesque plot
The serious vied with grim absurdity
   And tears with smiles were tangled in a knot.

Of all the features in our history
   This seemed the worst: that after all was done,
The tears and smiles had touched her evenly,
   I gained a heritage of tears alone.

XXXII

Enveloped in her beauty, she passed by,
  I let her pass in graceful dignity;
Nor turned to glance at her with wistful eye,
  Though something whispered to me: "This is
    she."

Who hath re-joined the eve with morning's light?
  I do not know the underlying cause;
I know, though, that in one brief summer-night,
  Both twilights were united and "It was."

XXXIII

It was an argument of words alone,
  Yet you and I will never quite agree
As a result of our perplexity
  Who should in justice call the fault his own.

It is unfortunate, that love has not
  A dictionary, wherein one might see,
When pride is merely pride and when it ought
  To be construed as proper dignity.

XXXIV

Wordless she crosses and in every limb
   Breathes silent harmony; her foot-steps sound
   And, sounding, they recall the measured round
And rhythmic cadence of a volant hymn.

As leisurely her eyes half-opened turn,
   Those eyes as clear as day within her face,
   The earth and sky as much as they embrace,
With fresher lustre in her pupils burn.

She laughs; her laughter has the rippling notes
   Of flowing waters, which the hearers bless;
She weeps; each tear a poem, which promotes
   An endless flood of soothing tenderness.

Possessed is she of perfume and of light,
   Of pleasing lines and colors fair to see;
She has the form, which the desires invite
   And the expression, — fount of poetry.

That she is stupid? — Bah! While silence shields
   That dark enigma, I'll maintain: to me
There is more value in what she conceals,
   Than in another girl's loquacity.

XXXV

I'm not amazed at thy forgetfulness.
I marvelled much more, that thou couldst profess
Affection for me, even for a day;
For, that there is a latent quality
In me, which challenges the world's respect,
—Thy inexperience could not detect.

XXXVI

If a record of our injuries were written in a book
And from our souls we could them all as readily
    efface, as
This chronicle of grievances upon the page erases,—
I love you still so fondly and such deep and lasting
    traces
Were left within my breast by love, that if you un-
    dertook
To blot one, single injury, however trivial,
I, through your generous attitude, would gladly
    blot them all.

XXXVII

Before thee I shall die: for now I feel
   By thy hand dealt without a warning sound,
Within my bowels, the remorseless steel
   Which opened up the wide and deadly wound.

Before thee I shall die: my spirit will
   Serenely seated, with expectant faith,
Tenacious in its perseverance still,
   Await thy coming at the gates of Death.

Thus will by hours, the days have swiftly passed,
   By days, the years precipitately flee
And at yon portal thou wilt call at last, —
   Who is exempt from this fatality?

Then may the earth thy short-comings conceal
   And shield thy faults from scrutinizing blame,
And may the waves of Death all sin and shame
   Like to another Jordan cleanse and heal.

There, where the murmurs of existence wend
   Their trembling way to death with spent desire,
Just as the ocean-billows find their end
   Upon the shore and silently expire;

There, where the grave, which closes o'er the dead
   Opens the portals of eternity, —
There shall we speak, without reserve or dread
   To mock our former taciturnity!

XXXVIII

Sighs are but air and vanish into air;
Tears are but water, flowing to the sea,
When love's forgotten, tell me, woman, where
It goes to, vanishing in mystery.

XXXIX

Why tell me of it? I perceive it well. —
She is capricious, haughty, changeable,
Vain as a peacock and I know, before
A spark of feeling issues from her heart,
The waters from a barren rock will pour
And life unto the desert sands impart.

I know her heart is but a serpent nest
Wherein no fibre may respond to love;
She is a lifeless statue at the best,
Whom admiration cannot warm nor move.
Yet — after all her faults are cited — who'll
Deny, that she is wondrous beautiful?

XL

God knows alone, how many times we too
Have idly strolled beneath the lofty elms
That lent her house an air of mystery
And shade unto the portico. — Her hand
In both of mine; her eyes fixed on my own;
Her head upon my shoulder in repose. —
— And yesterday — (A year had passed since then,
Just like a puff of air), — how self-possessed,
How inexpressibly composed she seemed,
As she with admirable calmness said,
When an officious friend presented me:
"It seems to me, that we have met before."

Ye scandal-mongering, pompous dowagers,
And leaders of good tone, — what you have missed,
Since you pursue the fascinating sport
Of heart-entanglement! — A choicer bit
Of savory gossip could not be devised,
A dainty morsel, which you could devour
In chorus, "sotto voce," and behind
Your waving fans of ostrich-plumes and gold.

O moon, oft vaunted as discreet and chaste!
Ye elms, the murm'ring guardians of our love!
O walls, that sheltered us in days of yore!
Shade of the portico; — Be silent! — May
The secret now not find you indiscreet.
Be silent, I implore; I have forgot
My part of it — and she? — There is no mask
So coldly non-committal as her face.

XLI

You are the hurricane and I the tower
Which rigid and impassive, mocks your power;
Your fury would uproot me where I stand
And scatter me in fragments o'er the land;
      It could not be.

You are the ocean, I, the massive rock,
Which, stolid and impervious, meets the shock;
You would delight to lift me from my base
And cast me headlong, prostrate on my face;
      It could not be.

You beautiful, I proud; your nature steeled
To conquer others, my own not to yield;
Our path confined; — a blockhead could foretell
A fierce concussion unavoidable.
      It could not be.

XLII

When they informed me of my deep distress,
  I felt the entrance of a blade of steel.
  I leaned against a wall; could dimly feel
How I lost memory and consciousness.

Night fell upon my spirit, — sombre, deep;
  In my impiety and anger's fill
  My soul then understood, how one can kill,
It comprehended, how a man can weep.

The cloud of grief swept by; my vigor bore it;
  Who brought to me the dismal news, you ask?
  It was a friend, who undertook the task.
It was a favor — and I thanked him for it.

XLIII

The light I placed on one side, then sat down
　　Upon the edge of the disordered bed;
Silent and motionless, with deep-set frown
　　And staring eyes, expressionless and dead.

How long a time I sat there? I don't know,
But when the heavy incubus of woe
Had passed in grim procession, I could see
The sunlight streaming on my balcony.

I cannot tell, what passed in stern review
　　Within my brain, that night of grief and rage;
I wept and cursed and felt within me, too,
　　The first true symptoms of declining age.

XLIV

As in an open book I clearly read
　　The very bottom of your pupils. Need
Your laughing lips indulge in useless lies,
So plainly contradicted by your eyes?

Weep then, nor deem it falsely as a shame,
That you were once a little fond of me;
Weep! No one sees us. I'm a man — and see!
I weep as well and would be more to blame.

XLV

Upon the loosened keystone of the arch
   Whose efflorescence time has stained with red
Rude Gothic artisans, whose names long dead,
   Carved an escutcheon, which the seasons parch.

Its granite helmet flourishes a crest
   Of verdant ivy, twined with graceful art,
Lending its shadows to the shield at rest,
   Where, grasped within a hand, appears a heart.

At seeing this in the deserted square
   We halted and she said to me: "Above
Yon ruined arch, behold engraven there
   The fitting emblem of my constant love."

Those were the words she spoke. — Alas they were
   Significant, as I can well attest:
The heart was borne within the hand by her
   And everywhere, except within the breast.

XLVI

In shadows skulking, from behind she wounded me,
Her base betrayal sealing with a traitor's kiss;
Her arms around my neck entwined, a feigned caress,
She pierced my heart, with calm, cold-blooded cruelty.

Yet joyfully her way pursuant is she found
Unmoved, impassive, happy, smiling, gay and why?
Because no tell-tale blood-drops trickle from the wound
Because he walks about, who, none the less must die.

XLVII

I have ascended many a lofty peak
    Where earthly realms commingled with the sky
Nor, for an instant, did my heart grow weak
    While gauging their proportions with my eye.

Of late I gazed into a heart's abyss
    And shuddered and drew backward with a cry
When I beheld that awful precipice, —
    So vast and black was its profundity.

XLVIII

As, from a wound, one tears the dripping steel,
  So from my heart I tore my hapless love,
Although I felt, that by this act I drove
  All joy from life as well, without repeal.

From my soul's altar, reared with loving care,
  My will cast down her image with disdain;
The ardent light of faith enkindled there
  Extinguished quite in the deserted fane.

And still, at times, her vision in my mind
  To combat with my resolution seems, —
When will it come, the time, when I shall find
  The placid slumbers which prohibit dreams.

XLIX

Sometimes I meet her in the world and she
Seems unconcerned and passes smilingly;
While I harass my aching brain the while:
"How is it possible, that she can smile!"

Another smile then rises to my lip,
A badge of grief, effectively to nip
All curious comment, and at once I feel:
"Perhaps she smiles as I do — to conceal."

L

That, which the savage, who with skilless hand
  Makes from a log at his caprice a God
Then bows the knee before the work he planned,
  That you and I accomplished and applaud.

True forms we gave to phantasy's device,
  A ludicrous invention of the brain;
The idol now complete, we sacrifice
  Our love upon its altar and in vain.

LI

Of the small remnant of my life still due
I'd gladly give the happiest year or two,
Could I but learn, with any certainty,
What you have said to others about me.

And all my earthly life and what I'd gain
From an eternal one, (should I gain ought),
I'd sacrifice, if I could ascertain,
  What you of me in solitude have thought.

LII

Gigantic waves, that break with sullen roar
Upon the distant and deserted shore,
In foam-sheets wrapped, tumultuous and hoar,
    O bear me with you!

Force of the hurricane, whose gusts surprise
The shrivelled leaf, which in the forest dies,
In blind gyrations dragging off its prize,
    O bear me with you!

Clouds of the tempest, which the lightnings break,
Whose ragged borders fire adorns, — to make
Among the sombre mists a startling wake,
    O bear me with you!

Bear me, in pity, where, with reason, may
A dizzy whirl tear out my memory, —
In pity! — For I tremble to remain
Alone within a wilderness of pain!

LIII

The dusky swallows will return again
  To build their nests upon your balcony,
Flutter their pinions at your window-pane
  And, seeking entrance, greet you playfully.

But, those same birds, who used to pause in flight
  To marvel at your beauty and to yearn
For bliss like mine; who knew our names and sight
  Those birds, alas, will not again return.

The swelling honey-suckles once more will
  Ascend the trellis of your garden-wall;
Again, at even-tide, their flowers will fill
  The air with fragrance, sweet and mystical.

But those, o'erladen with nocturnal dew,
  Whose drops we saw to glisten, tremble, fall, —
Like day-light tears, — these neither I nor you
  Will ever be enabled to recall.

Within your ears, the ardent tones of love
  Will sound again; perchance, your heart will leap
In glad response and that the charm may prove
  A sweet awakening from protracted sleep.

But, — mute, absorbed, and kneeling, — as we see
  The pious worshipper his God adore, —
— As I have loved you once! — Nay, credit me,
  No one will ever love you any more!

LIV

Whene'er we venture to invoke the past,
  Those fleeting hours, so lifeless now and sere,
  In her black lashes shines a trembling tear,
Ready to fall, by tender griefs amassed;

  And falls at last, like sparkling drop of dew,
    At contemplating which, we realize,
  That present sighs to yesterday are due
    And that tomorrow for the present sighs.

LV

Amid the orgy's shrill, discordant din
My hearing was caressed, though no one nigh,
As with the tender echo of a sigh
To far-off notes of music close akin.

The echo of a sigh, which I know well,
Formed of a breath, which to my thirst appealed,
The perfume of a flower, grown concealed
Within the shadows of a cloister's cell.

My sweetheart of the moment lovingly
Inquired: "Where are your thoughts?" — "No-
    where," said I;
"Nowhere, and you are weeping?" — "O, I had
"A merry sadness and the wine is sad."

LVI

To-day like yesterday, to-morrow like to-day,
A drear succession of monotony;
The same gray sky, a limitless expanse,
The ever-ready impulse to advance.

The heart in motion like a measured tread
Seems but a stupid, regular machine;
Our dull intelligence lives on in dread,
Skulking in corners, fearful to be seen.

The soul, ambitious for a paradise,
Seeks without faith, accepts fatigue without
A goal; nor knows the wave, which wheels about,
Why it engages in the enterprise.

A voice, which in unceasing monotone
Drones off a litany's incessant clause;
Persistent drop of water on the stone,
Which falls and falls, without a moment's pause.

Thus are the days unravelled, one by one,
Successive in a long and dreary chain;
To-day the same as yesterday has gone
Without distinctive traits of joy or pain.

Alas, at times, I wistfully recall
My former griefs and I would gladly give
The present for the past! — True, grief is gall,
But, none the less, to suffer is to live.

LVII

This worn-out scaffolding of skin and bones
Grows weary finally to promenade
A madman's head, nor do I wonder much;
For though 't is true, that time's defacing touch
Not yet with years upon my prime has preyed,
Yet, to my harm, a worldly life atones;
I 've made such use of it, that I might say
An age has been condensed within each day.

Thus, even if I at this moment died
I could not truly claim, I had not lived;
Though new appears the garment's outward pride,
I know within, that age has been achieved.

Yes, I 've grown old, thanks to my luckless star!
My sad solicitude so tells me now;
There is a pain, which, passing, leaves its scar
Graved in the heart, if not upon the brow.

LVIII

Do you desire, that this delicious nectar
Shall not disgust you with its bitter lees?
Well, then, imbibe it, sip with cautious palate
And then abandon all its witcheries.

Do you desire, that both of us shall cherish
A grateful mem'ry of our passion's spell?
Let us, to-day, adore each other madly
And, on the morrow, calmly say: "Farewell."

LIX

I know the reason for your longing sighs,
I know, too, where your cause for languor lies.
You smile? Some day, my girl, like I
You'll know the reason why;
You now, perhaps, suspect it,
And I detect it.

I know your dreams and what in dreams you see,
Read on your brow, what you conceal from me.
You smile? Some day, my girl, like I
You'll know the reason why;
You now, perhaps, suspect it,
And I detect it!

I know why tears and smiles at once control
I penetrate your guarded virgin soul.
You smile? Some day, my girl, like I
You'll know the reason why;
While you feel much and know but little, — I
Who nothing feel, know all your history.

LX

My life is a desert;
  The flowers I touch
Lose petals and wither.
  The mischief is such,
As if in my pathway
  Some foe seeded evil,
So that I might harvest
  The crop of the devil.

LXI

To see my hours of fever and the bane
Of sleepless vigils pass and rest denied, —
Who is the faithful one to sit beside
     My couch of pain?

When I extend my hand in parting grasp
At death's approaching tremulous, — but still
Seeking a friendly hand, — Whose pressure will
     Return its clasp?

When death's inexorable dictum bids
The crystals of my eyes to vitrify, —
Who'll close, to cover up the broken eye
     My staring lids?

When tolls the deep-toned church-bell solemnly,
(If at my funeral, a bell should toll)
When prayers are said for the departing soul,
     — Who'll pray for me?

When now my pallid remnants calmly sleep
Pressed down by earth within a narrow cave,
Above my lonely and forgotten grave, —
     Who'll come to weep?

And who, at length, when he again will see
The brilliant sun its wonted orbit fill,
Shall in his worldly occupations still
     Remember me?

LXII

At first a vague and trembling streak of gray,
  A restless flash of light which cuts the sea;
Soon after sparkles, grows and spreads the day
  In ardent outbursts of transparency.

The brilliant lustre is our inward joy,
  The timorous shadow is our sorrow's weight;
When will that dawn, which has so long been coy
  The gloomy night within my soul elate?

LXIII

Like a swarm of irritated bees
In a persecuting phalanx massed,
From my mem'ry's dim obscurities
Throng the recollections of the past.

I would fly. — 'T is useless; I 'm their goal.
They surround me, buzz about, — advance;
In succession each one quickly plants
That sharp poniard, which inflames the soul.

LXIV

As the miser guards his treasure,
  I'm my sorrow's sentinel;
I would demonstrate with pleasure,
  That within us there might dwell
Some eternal quality
Like the love she swore to me.

But to-day I call in vain
  For the grief, which passed away
And I hear its voice complain:
  "Wretched, miserable clay,
"Far too fickle to maintain
"Constancy in misery!"

LXV

The night drew on; I found no shelter nigh;
And I was thirsty, — so I drank my tears;
And I was hungry and beset with fears;
I closed my swollen eyes, — that I might die.

I was within a desert, — though the sound
Of hoarsely-seething crowds roared like the sea;
— Orphaned and poor, — instinctively I found:
The world was a deserted place — for me.

LXVI

Whence do I come? Seek thou the roughest
    trail,
Of foot-paths the most horrible; the trace
Of bloody footprints on the flinty stone;
A soul despoiled, in tatters and disgrace;
These signs pursue; thy efforts will not fail.
The brier's stubborn prickles will alone
Infallibly direct thee on the way
Unto the cradle of my history.

Where go I now? Across a comfortless,
A desolate and darkened wilderness;
A pallid vale of everlasting snow,
Where endless, melancholy winters blow;
To where a solitary, nameless stone
Is as a landmark to the dead unknown;
Where dwells forgetfulness in silent gloom,
There shall I find, and there alone, my tomb.

LXVII

How beautiful to see the day
   With crown of fire arise and flush,
How, at his kiss of light, display
   The waves their lustre, air its blush!

How beautiful, when autumn showers
   Are followed by a dark-blue sky,
To breathe at eve, of dampened flowers
   The fragrance to satiety!

How beautiful, when softly fall
   In pure white flakes the silent snow,
To see like red tongues in the hall
   The restless flames astir and glow!

How beautiful, are dozing dreams,
   To sleep well, — as sub-deacons snore,
To eat and gorge one's self, — it seems
   A pity we should ask for more!

LXVIII

I do not know now what I dreamt last night,
  Sad, very sad, my visions must have been
  For after I awoke, I felt within
My anxious dread, how durable my plight.

More self-possessed, regaining my control,
  I saw the moistened pillow where I slept,
  And for the first time felt, because I wept,
A bitter sense of joy invade my soul.

Sad is that sleep which waits on misery
  Which artful may our pent-up griefs decoy,
  Yet has my sadness one consoling joy,
I know, that tears are not denied to me.

LXIX

As in a flash of lightning we are born
And even while its brightness lasts, we die:
So brief is our existence here beneath!

The love and glory we pursue are shorn
Like shadowy dreams of all reality:
And the awakening from the dream is death!

LXX

How often I, close to the moss grown walls
Which guard her peace, (an unseen sentinel),
Have heard at mid of night the tinkling bell,
Which all her sisterhood to matins calls.

How often has the silvered moonlight traced
My mournful shadow, when the seamed and tall
Funereal cypress topped the garden-wall;
How often there our shadows have embraced!

And when about the church night's shadows fell,
How often have I seen the lamplight gleam,
Vibrating o'er the panes, a grateful beam
Within the ogive window of her cell!

What though the wind might whistle through the
    tower
In dusky corners with frenetic ire,
I heard her penetrant, sweet voice o'erpower
All other voices in the sacred choir.

On winter nights, if some one with a face
More bold, than others', o'er the lonely square
Would try to cross and saw me standing there
He lost no time in quickening his pace.

And old crones were not wanting, who would spin
The dreadful gossip with their morning bowl,
That I was certainly some sexton's soul,
Who died impenitent, in pride of sin.

In perfect gloom, my sense of place complete,
Each corner of the porch and portal knew;
The nettles, which in wild abundance grew
Preserved, perhaps, the imprints of my feet.

The owls, alarmed at first, whose eyes of flame
Pursued in darkness my temerity,
Became resigned in course of time, to see
In me a comrade and grew very tame.

Quite close at hand, the reptiles silently,
Moved as they pleased, without a moment's awe;
And even the mute and granite saints I saw,
Saluted me with stately courtesy.

LXXI

I did not sleep;—within that limbo state
   I loitered, where all objects change their form;
Mysterious spaces, meant to separate
   Our dreamland fancies from the wakeful norm.

My thoughts, which had been in a noiseless round
   Of whirls within the circuit of my brain,
Little by little in their dance were found
   To fall into a gentler pace again.

The eyelids watched the reflex of the light
   Which to the soul found entrance through the
      eyes,
But, from within, another flame made bright
   The world of visionary ecstasies.

Just at this point there sounded in my ear
   A murmur similar in pitch, as when
One may the faithful in the temple hear
   To terminate their prayers with Amen.

I heard, as if a voice, with sadness blent
   Had called me by my name from far away;
And felt the snuffed-out waxy tapers' scent,
   Of moisture and of incense vapors gray.

The night came on and, wearied, I fell prone
   In sleep's embrace, unconscious as a stone;
When from deep slumber I awoke, I cried:
   "Some one, whom I have dearly loved, has
      died!"

Limbo: region bordering on hell

LXXII

First Voice

The billows have a latent harmony,
A dainty scent the violet in the grove,
A silv'ry rime the frosty nights display,
While gold and light are properties of day;
But I have something all these things above,
— For I have love.

Second Voice

Applauding current, radiating cloud,
An envious wave, professing to adore you,
An isle of dreams, to phantasy endowed,
Where rests the weary spirit, anxious-browed,
A sweet intoxication transitory,
    Is human glory!

Third Voice

A glowing cinder is the lust for treasure,
A flying shadow is our vanity;
Renown and gold and all are lies, in measure,
The only thing, which gives me lasting pleasure,
I say it with regard to verity:
    Is liberty!

Thus the boatmen passed by, singing
Their eternal barcarole;
With the foam against the oar-stroke springing
While the glaring sun surveyed the whole.

"Wilt thou embark with us?" — they cried to me;
But I said, smiling, as they passed me by:
"Some time ago I did; you still may see
"My clothing on the beach, stretched out to dry."

LXXIII

They closed the fixed and staring eyes
Which had been open until now
And covered with a snowy cloth
The gentle face and pallid brow;
Some sobbed, while some in silence went
Out of that mournful tenement.

The light, which burned within a glass
Upon the floor, beside the pall
Cast disproportioned shadows of
The bed upon the chamber-wall;
At times one could distinctly see
The body outlined rigidly.

When daylight came in streaks of gray
The world awoke with wonted noise;
Before that startling counterpoise
Of light and shade, — life, mystery,
By melancholy quite subdued
And grave reflections moved, I said:
"My God, into what solitude
"Do we consign our dead!"

They bore her on their shoulders from
The house into the temple, where
They placed her on a catafalque
Within a chapel; — left her there,
With yellow tapers' company
And sable folds of drapery.

And when the bells at eventide
Their last notes to the faithful gave,
An ancient crone said her last prayer
And crossed the solitary nave.
The portals creak, deserted is
The huge and sacred edifice.

One heard the measured pendulum
Vibrating in the belfry clock,
The fitful sputtering of wax
Seemed to the silence like a shock;
With dread and listlessness imbued
I, trembling in the darkness, said:
"My God, into what solitude
"Do we consign our dead!"

Revolving in the lofty tower
The iron-tongued and solemn bell
Gave her to speed her on her way
Its last and pitiful farewell.
Friends and relations form in line
In mourning to escort her shrine.

The pickaxe opened up a niche
Confined and dark, close to the wall,
And there they laid her tenderly
And covered her and left her all, —
One reminiscent, last salute
And grief departed, or was mute.

The sexton, shouldering his pick,
Went off and soon was lost to sight
I heard him singing through his teeth;
Then came the advent of the night,
Deep silence reigned, the shadows strewed
Their veils about me, as I said:
"My God, into what solitude
"Do we consign our dead!"

In long and frozen winter-nights,
When timbers creak before the gale
When lash the trembling window panes
The furious gusts of sleet and hail,
My heart recalls with dismal groan
The poor girl sleeping there alone.

There falls the rain's eternal sound
In dripping, dreary monotone;
The tempest's breath perhaps disturbs
Her rest, abandoned and alone;
Close to the stone-wall, green with mould,
Perhaps her bones are chilled with cold!

Does dust return to dust? And does
The soul fly upward to the sky?
Or else, is all vile matter, which
Decays, and is condemned to die?
I know not, but I can't explain
That something which imparts to me
Alike repugnancy and pain,
To think, that we should calmly see,
Our dead consigned to such a rude,
Relentless, mournful solitude!

LXXIV

Their robes ungirt with dignity sedate,
   Extracted from its sheath the flaming sword,
Upon the golden threshold of the gate
   Two angels stood on guard.

As toward the iron staves I ventured near,
   The entrance warding, — I saw, as I blinked
Through double rows of gratings in the rear,
   Her, white and indistinct.

I saw her, just as one an image might
   In light and non-oppressive dreams see pass;
Like a diffused and slender ray of light
   Swims in a dark morass.

I felt my soul seized with a fierce desire;
   As an abyss attracts with fearful yawn,
So towards this mystery, my mind afire,
   I felt myself drawn on.

But, woe is me! The angels indicate
   By their expression, that this hope is dross;
It seems to say: "The threshold of this gate
   "No one but God may cross!"

LXXV

May it be true, that, when our eyes are tipped
   By slumber's rosy fingers, — soars in flight
The soul, from its residing prison slipped,
   To empyrean height?

May it be true, that on a gust of air
   It rises, winged, the guest of mists, into
An empty space, nocturnal breezes lair,
   For general rendezvous?

And, that, denuded of its human guise
   It has, for brief hours, as asylum sought
The realm, where broken all terrestrial ties,
   The silent world of thought?

And laughs and weeps and hates and loves, and keeps
   For souvenir a trail of joy and pain,
As when a meteor in grandeur sweeps
   Across the heavenly plain?

I do not know, if this strange world of dreams
   May live without, or from within us flow;
But many people do I know, it seems,
   Whom yet I do not know.

LXXVI

I saw in the imposing nave of the Byzantine dome
Within its dim, uncertain light, an ancient Gothic tomb;
The trembling rays through colored panes accentuate the gloom.

A book within her hands, which are enfolded o'er her breast,
A beauteous woman o'er an urn recumbent, is at rest;
The chisel, which produced that form, ranked surely with the best.

The rigid couch of granite swelled with softened fold and plait,
As if it were of tender down and satin delicate,
In which her comely body sank its non-resisting weight.

The face preserved of its last smile, a radiant effigy,
Just as the Western sky retains the glories of the day,
Whene'er the dying sun has spent his final, furtive ray.

Two angels sat within a row, whose obvious intent
Beside her stony pillow, on their lips a finger bent,
To caution reverent silence in the calm environment.

She seemed not dead, but sleeping there, as she
  reposeful lies
Beneath the massive arches and half-shadowed
  canopies;
And in her dreams she seemed to have a view of
  Paradise.

I cautiously approached the sombre corner of the
  nave,
As men with muffled footstep and with bated
  breath behave,
When they, beside a cradle, would an infant's
  slumber save.

I looked at her a moment, as she with gentle grace
Reclined upon her couch of stone, and at the
  glorious face
And where, beside her, near the wall, remained a
  vacant space.

And in my soul was roused to life that infinite
  desire,
Which burns within this life of death, like latent,
  anxious fire,
To gain that life, where centuries like instances
  transpire.

Fatigued with endless combats, in which I, wrest-
  ling, live,
I sometimes think with envy of her calm alterna-
  tive,
Of that placid, hidden corner, — like a mental
  sedative.

That mute and pallid woman at intervals will dwell
In mind and then I say: "Death loves us silently and well;
"How tranquil must her slumber be within that narrow cell!"